What could it be?!

As Benjamin [...] fade away into t[...]ced something sti[...] the water's surface, close to the horizon.

His backpack was in the car, but he'd brought his binoculars in case there were any interesting birds to watch. They were strapped around his neck and tucked under his old T-shirt for protection. Benjamin took them out and focused on where he'd seen the movement. For a moment, he saw only a huge expanse of water—then he saw some splashing and the flash of a gray body leaping out!

Could it be a whale? he wondered. Maybe he would finally see one!

Books in the Jeff Corwin Series

JUNIOR EXPLORER SERIES: BOOK 4

A WHALE
OF A TIME!

Illustrations by Guy Francis

PUFFIN BOOKS
An Imprint of Penguin Group (USA) Inc.

To Natasha, Maya,
and Marina

PUFFIN BOOKS
Published by the Penguin Group
Penguin Young Readers Group, 345 Hudson Street, New York, New York 10014, U.S.A.
Penguin Group (Canada), 90 Eglinton Avenue East, Suite 700, Toronto, Ontario, Canada M4P 2Y3
(a division of Pearson Penguin Canada Inc.)
Penguin Books Ltd, 80 Strand, London WC2R 0RL, England
Penguin Ireland, 25 St Stephen's Green, Dublin 2, Ireland (a division of Penguin Books Ltd)
Penguin Group (Australia), 250 Camberwell Road, Camberwell, Victoria 3124, Australia
(a division of Pearson Australia Group Pty Ltd)
Penguin Books India Pvt Ltd, 11 Community Centre, Panchsheel Park, New Delhi - 110 017, India
Penguin Group (NZ), 67 Apollo Drive, Rosedale, Auckland 0632, New Zealand
(a division of Pearson New Zealand Ltd.)
Penguin Books (South Africa) (Pty) Ltd, 24 Sturdee Avenue,
Rosebank, Johannesburg 2196, South Africa

Registered Offices: Penguin Books Ltd, 80 Strand, London WC2R 0RL, England

Published by Puffin Books, a division of Penguin Young Readers Group, 2011

Copyright © Jeff Corwin, 2010
All rights reserved

ISBN 978-0-14-241646-4

Printed at R.R. Donnelley & Sons
Bloomsburg, PA
May 2011

Dear Reader,

Before my family moved to a rural part of Massachusetts, I grew up outside of Boston, where I wasn't always able to explore the natural world. So I had to find unique ways to discover the animals and plants around me—which led me right into my backyard! Even though I was living in a city, I found lots of amazing wildlife right outside my door. I just had to take a closer look!

And that's what the Baxter kids like to do in my Junior Explorer series—explore their immediate surroundings. Whether at the beach or in their hometown near the Florida Everglades, Lucy and Benjamin Baxter always find ways to discover fascinating animals and plants. And so can you! It doesn't matter where you live—all you have to do is look outside, engage your curiosity about the natural world, and have fun discovering the plants, animals, and natural life around you.

Happy exploring!

Jeff Corwin

JEFF CORWIN

A WHALE
OF A TIME!

Chapter One

Benjamin Baxter wasn't taking any chances with his mint-chip ice-cream cone. It was the first time he'd been allowed to get a double scoop! So as his family began window-shopping in Woods Hole, a village in Cape Cod, Massachusetts, he kept one eye on his ice cream at all times.

With his other eye, he was taking in his surroundings. The Baxters had just arrived, and they'd decided to go on a tour of the area after quickly checking into their motel. Woods Hole had a quaint main street lined with weather-beaten wooden buildings that looked like they'd been there for hundreds of years, and it seemed like every other street led right to the ocean.

As the Baxters walked around, Benjamin's parents were in full tour-guide mode. "Cape Cod is a peninsula that juts off the eastern shore of Massachusetts," said Mrs. Baxter as they passed an antique shop. "People say that it looks like an arm sticking out into the Atlantic, flexing its muscles and ending with a clenched fist. If you imagine it that way, then Woods Hole is at the shoulder, close to the mainland."

Benjamin craned his neck for a glimpse of the ocean glinting in the afternoon sun. It was sprinkled with sailboats and motorboats, and he saw what looked like a ferry. He couldn't wait to get down to the harbor for a closer look! Instead, his mom and dad seemed to be peering into every shop they passed.

"Cape Cod is well-known for its beaches," his dad continued, "but it's also full of history. Did you know that the Pilgrims came here first, before they made their way to Plymouth Rock? And there are more lighthouses here than in any other county in the country."

Benjamin crunched his ice-cream cone. "Cool!" he said. "But how about, you know . . ."

He and his sister, Lucy, liked history as much as any kid, but what they *really* liked was science. That was their dad's main interest, too, but they didn't usually visit such historic places. Benjamin had to get him back to the most important questions. "What animals live here? Where? And when can we see them?" he asked.

His dad smiled. "Cape Cod is teeming with wildlife," he said. "Whales and dolphins live in the nearby waters, plus many kinds of shellfish. Lobsters, of course. Not to mention the seabirds and other animals that make the sand dunes their home. Many of the towns on the Cape started out as fishing villages. But now tourism is the biggest industry. Building and development—

in addition to the natural forces of wind and water—are changing the landscape of the Cape. Development is having a similar effect back home in Florida. That's a little bit of what I'll be talking about in my lecture tomorrow," he added.

Mr. Baxter was delivering a guest lecture at the Woods Hole Research Center the next day, comparing environmental changes in the Everglades with changes on the Cape. Benjamin was always proud of his father's work, and especially proud that he'd been invited here to talk about it. Several of the world's best-known centers for ocean science were right here in Woods Hole! The only problem was that Benjamin was a little worried his dad's work would get in the way of his own plans: seeing all the wildlife. "After your lecture, we'll go to the beach, right?" he asked anxiously. "Check out the tide pools and the dunes? Maybe we can even see a whale?" He still remembered the humpback he'd caught sight of in Alaska. It was really amazing to see something so huge pop out of the water. As big as the whale was, the sighting lasted only a few seconds— and left Benjamin hungry for more!

"We have to!" Lucy chimed in.

His father chuckled. "We'll try. Remember, though, this is just a quick trip. As soon as the weekend is over, it's back to Florida and back to school!"

Suddenly, Mrs. Baxter changed the subject. "Here we are," she said brightly, as they stopped in front of what looked like a church. "Anyone want to visit the scientific community of Woods Hole?"

"Yes!" Benjamin and Lucy said together. Benjamin quickly finished his cone, and they followed Mrs. Baxter in.

As they walked through the church doors, a giant whale's tail greeted them. "Welcome to the exhibit center of the Woods Hole Oceanographic Institution!" Mr. Baxter exclaimed. Lucy and Ben looked at each other and grinned. The inside of the church had been completely made over, and where the pews had been, there were now exhibits about the institute's amazing work. "Since this facility is

so close to the water, expeditions set off from here to map the ocean floor, study the properties of the water, and discover the secrets of the deep," their dad explained.

As Benjamin took it all in, an exhibit about marine mammals caught his attention. "Hey, Lucy, look over here," he said excitedly, as he ran over to the display. Lucy joined him. "It says here that researchers discovered new details about how dolphins use sounds to travel large distances with their pods," Lucy said, reading a sign on the wall. "Scientists tracked the dolphins by attaching equipment to their fins."

Benjamin really wanted to see some dolphins while they were here. There were dolphins back home in Florida, but were they different from the ones in Cape Cod? Did they behave differently? Benjamin wanted to find out! "Maybe we could search for dolphins, too, when your lecture is over?" he asked his dad hopefully. Being in this exhibit center was reminding him of everything he wanted to do.

"Sounds like a great idea," his dad replied, "if we can fit it in." Before he could get more specific, his cell phone's ringtone filled the quiet room. "Excuse me," he said apologetically to the museum attendant as he flipped open his phone. "Yes, this is Sam Baxter." He turned his back to the kids, and Benjamin figured he was ironing out some last-minute details for his lecture.

His mom was absorbed in another exhibit, so Benjamin went looking for Lucy. She had wandered over to some sort of tiny ship. He'd never seen anything like it. "What's this?" Benjamin asked as he walked up to Lucy.

"It's a small submarine that fits three people and can dive almost three miles beneath the surface of the ocean! This is an exact replica of the sub that many Woods Hole scientists have used on their missions," she explained.

"Wow!" said Benjamin excitedly. He didn't realize anyone had heard him until he saw the museum attendant walking toward him and Lucy. "You can go inside, you know," she said.

The Baxter kids squeezed in behind the control panel while the attendant told them more about the vehicle. "It's called the *Alvin*, and it's made more than four thousand dives!" she

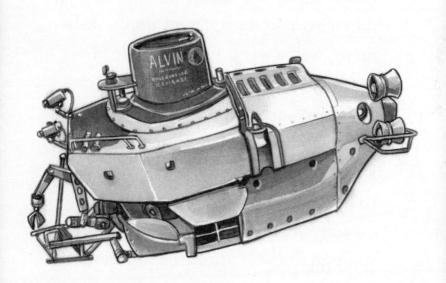

explained. "We have other research vessels, too, larger ships that stay at the surface of the water. But the *Alvin* is special because it takes scientists—not just their tools—to the bottom of the ocean."

"What do they do down there?" Benjamin asked.

"They observe and photograph different species," the attendant said. "And, using the craft's robotic arms, they also take samples of rocks, sediment, water—you name it. The *Alvin* has made dozens of major discoveries. Scientists find that it's easier to understand connections between different kinds of sea life when they see it face to face."

Lucy was reading the signs that were placed all over the interior of the sub. "The *Alvin* helped explore the wreckage of the *Titanic*?" she asked, fascinated.

The museum attendant smiled. "It did some of the first investigations," she said. "You've probably seen pictures from its trips. Inside the *Alvin*, explorer Robert Ballard was the first person to get close to the *Titanic* since it sank in 1912."

Lucy's eyes were wide. "Can you imagine visiting the ocean floor?" she said to Benjamin. "It would be like going to outer space!"

"I'd settle for just seeing the ocean up close at this point," Benjamin said. This museum was cool, but he really wanted to get near the water.

Just then, their mom and dad walked up to the exhibit. "I would love to go down in the *Alvin* myself!" Mr. Baxter told the attendant, smiling. "If these kids would make some room for me!"

Benjamin and Lucy giggled and shuffled over as their dad climbed into the pilot's seat next to them. "Okay, you two," he said, turning to them and taking a more serious tone. "I know you're wondering what kind of exploring you can do while we're here, and believe it or not, I actually have a plan. I happen to know a fishing family here in town, and I've just finished firming up some details with them on the phone. It's not going underwater in a submersible, but how would you like to spend tomorrow on their fishing boat? They've offered to take you out while your mom and I are at the lecture."

Benjamin looked at Lucy, wondering if she was as excited as he was. No sitting in his dad's lecture with tons of grown-ups and their long questions. No more waiting and wondering what they were going to do. And maybe even a chance to see a whale up close! He jumped out of the *Alvin* model and pumped his fist in the air. They were going to see the Cape from the water—the best possible place. "Yes!" he yelled. "When do we leave?"

Chapter Two

At 8:00 a.m. the next morning, the Baxters stood on a small white boat in Woods Hole's harbor. "Benjamin, Lucy, this is Nina Simmons," Mr. Baxter said, clutching a paper cup of coffee. "She will be your guide for the morning!" Benjamin realized he'd seen pictures of Nina before. She'd gone to school with his dad, and she sent the Baxters a holiday card every year. Now

he remembered that she and her husband fished for lobster! He and Lucy were about to get an up close look at one of the animals Cape Cod was best known for.

"Hi there. Welcome aboard!" Nina said cheerfully. She was wearing a baseball cap and a sweatshirt, with a pair of waterproof overalls on top. "This is my husband, David," she said, pointing across the boat to a tall man in a similar outfit. David smiled and waved, then returned to the boat controls. "And this is my daughter, Addie," Nina said, ruffling the little girl's brown, curly hair. "School's closed today, so she's helping us out. She's seven, and she knows a lot about the ocean. She practically grew up on this boat!"

As Benjamin put on his life jacket, his eyes darted around. He saw the usual things you'd expect to find on a boat, like ropes and an anchor. But some other things surprised him: there were a number of what looked like cages, and some foam buoys. There was even a tank of water built into the deck! Benjamin couldn't wait to find out what all this stuff was for.

Benjamin and Lucy waved good-bye to their parents and called out "Good luck!" to their dad until the boat got too far away from the dock. "I'd have loved to hear his lecture," Nina said, "but I'm so happy to have some extra hands on deck!" While David steered the vessel from inside a small, roofed enclosure, Nina motioned for them to follow her.

She walked over to the pile of cages Benjamin had seen, and picked one up. "I'm not sure how much your dad has told you, but David and I fish in the waters between Cape Cod and Martha's Vineyard, using traps like these to catch lobster. This boat is specially equipped for storing them onboard until we can deliver them to markets and restaurants onshore. We were out here yesterday, setting traps, and now we need to check them to see what we've caught. Would you like to help me haul them up?"

Benjamin grinned. "Yes, please," he said. "As soon as you show me how!"

Addie piped up, "First we have to find our buoys. See how they're all different?" She pointed to the many buoys bobbing in the harbor, painted every color in the rainbow. "Each boat in this area has a different color," Addie explained. "And each buoy is attached to a trap. Our buoy color is pink, so if we find a pink one, we'll know where our trap is under the water." The boat zipped along for a while until Addie called out, "Oh! There's one, Dad!"

David steered the boat toward the buoy, and Nina grabbed it with a long stick. The buoy was attached to a rope, which she reeled in with a winch connected to the side of the boat. Benjamin and Lucy each got a chance to turn the reel, and before long, they could see the lobster trap coming up out of the water. Then Nina detached the trap from the pulley, placed it carefully on the deck, opened it, and took out a squirming lobster!

Nina held it up for a moment so Benjamin and Lucy could get a good look. It was about a foot long, with eight legs; two large claws; a long, narrow shell; and two pairs of antennae, one long and one short. It wasn't red, like Benjamin had expected, but rather a muddy green color. As if she'd read

Benjamin's mind, Nina said, "They turn red when they're cooked. But live lobsters come in many different colors, from black and brown to yellow and even blue!"

"I've never seen one up close before," Benjamin told her.

"Do they even live in Florida?" Lucy asked.

"A different type of lobster lives in the waters off Florida. That type, the spiny lobster, is usually clawless," Nina explained. "This lobster, as you can see, has two claws, one slightly larger than the other. The big one tears apart the shells of its prey, while the smaller one helps the lobster get to softer flesh inside."

As she talked about the claws, she

popped a rubber band on each of them.

"Why are you doing that?" Lucy asked.

"Rubber bands—for our safety and theirs," Nina answered, walking toward the tank Benjamin had seen before. "My catch will stay in this holding tank for now," she said, gently dropping the lobster in. "Soon there will be many lobsters in here, and while they are not normally aggressive animals, they will occasionally attack each other while in the tank. That's why we've banded their claws—to protect them from each other."

"Yikes!" said Benjamin. "Do they do that in the wild?"

Addie answered, since her mother had gone back to empty the rest of the trap. "Not usually. In their natural habitat, lobsters hide under rocks and use their antennae to find food. They mostly eat bottom dwellers, like clams and mussels and crabs. But sometimes they will prey on each other. The rubber bands just keep everyone safe."

Benjamin watched the lobster crawling around in the tank. Sure enough, its antennae waved around in the water, as if to sense what else was around. It used its legs to walk, and its tail stretched and contracted to help it move along. It reminded him of an insect, with its shell and many legs, but stronger and bigger. "How big do lobsters get?" he asked Addie.

She spread her arms out wide. "They

can get *really* big," she said. "People have found lobsters up to three feet long, and they can weigh up to forty pounds!"

"Wow, that's almost as heavy as our dog, Daisy," Benjamin said.

"And lobsters grow slowly," Addie continued, "shedding their shells as they get bigger, and the process never stops. If a lobster escapes predators, it can live for a very long time."

"This is really fascinating," Lucy said, grinning.

"And did you know that a lobster has the ability to drop a claw off if it's in danger?" Addie said, surprising Benjamin and Lucy with another cool fact. "The next time it sheds its shell, a new claw begins to grow back!"

"Are you sure?" Benjamin asked

doubtfully. "I thought starfish do that."

Addie nodded. "Lobsters do it, too. Most people just know they taste good, but they're amazing animals."

Nina came back with another trap she'd reeled in. "Look what we've got!" she said to the kids. "More lobsters, of course. Plus some crabs and even some sea urchins! The trap contains bait that attracts lobsters, but other animals tend to wander in," she explained. Carefully, she banded the lobsters and transferred them to the tank. "Does anyone want to take a look at a sea urchin before we send them back overboard?"

Nina reached into the tank, took out a pair of sea urchins, and carefully gave one to each of the Baxters.

Benjamin thought it would feel soft—it looked almost like a clover, round with a cloud of spines sticking out—but instead its spines were prickly. It didn't hurt, really, but it wasn't at all what he'd expected.

"Sea urchins live on the ocean floor, too," Addie said. "The spines protect them from predators. Check this out!"

She lightly touched one side of Benjamin's sea urchin, and all of its spines rippled toward the place where it had been touched.

Lucy did the same thing to her sea urchin, watching in wonder. "Wow!" she said.

As Nina located and pulled up the rest of the traps, the kids helped her throw the other sea life back into the water. Benjamin figured they were finished then, and he walked over to a corner of the deck, scanning the water for any sign of a whale. Would he ever see one again? he wondered. He was about to take out his binoculars when Lucy motioned him over to the rest of the group. They weren't done yet!

"Now we need to measure the lobsters," Addie said.

Lucy looked at her blankly. "What for?" she asked.

"To see which ones we can keep," Addie explained. "If a lobster is too small, we have to throw it back, just like we did with the crabs and the sea urchins."

"But why?" Benjamin wondered aloud. "I thought we were taking them back to shore."

"It's how we make sure that the lobster population stays healthy," Nina said. "We can't take them all if we want there to be more in the future!"

She picked up a lobster and measured its shell with a special ruler. "There are laws about how long a lobster's shell must be for us to keep it. Lobsters smaller than that are of breeding age. We want them to stay in the water, hatch more eggs, and keep the population growing. Sometimes we catch female lobsters, with eggs attached to their bodies—we throw those back, too," she added. "We do all we can to make sure that the lobster numbers will stay steady for years to come."

From inside his cabin, David added, "Sometimes nature helps us, too. The namesake fish of the Cape, the cod, is not as plentiful as it used to be. It's bad news for cod and cod fishermen, but good news for lobsters."

"Why?" asked Lucy.

"Cod are one of the greatest predators of the lobster," Nina explained.

"Really?" Benjamin couldn't help interrupting. "A fish can eat something that has claws?" He couldn't believe it!

Nina chuckled. "You'd be surprised. Cod can grow to three or even four feet long—they are much larger than your average lobster." Then she returned to Lucy's question. "Lobster populations

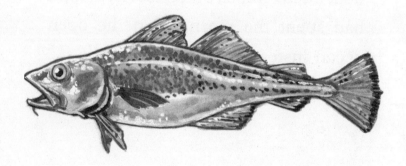

have been in decline as well, but with fewer cod, there is a better chance that the number of lobsters will grow again. There's no doubt that lobsters thrive when the cod population is down."

Benjamin thought this over as they made their way back to Woods Hole. His dad's lecture, he knew, was partly about how the many species of the Everglades depended on each other. And here they were talking about how the species of the North Atlantic depended on each other, too. Benjamin had spent the morning on the open ocean instead of at his dad's talk . . . and he hadn't missed a thing!

Chapter Three

After the morning on Nina's boat, anything else would seem a little boring, Benjamin thought. Still, there was nothing worse than slumping in the backseat of a too-small rental car stuck in traffic. It was Friday afternoon, and it seemed like everyone was at the Cape for the weekend. Mr. Baxter's lecture was over, and he wanted to take the family to the outer part of Cape Cod, the part that looked like a fist, for the next two nights. To get there, though, they had to drive along a congested road, and Benjamin saw more souvenir shops and miniature golf courses than wildlife habitats. "Trust me, this trip is well worth it," his mom said, sensing his frustration. "The Cape Cod National Seashore is not to be missed!"

After a while, the traffic finally thinned out, and Benjamin realized they might see some more of the natural world after all. Tall trees lined the road now, and when Lucy rolled down her window, he could even smell the salty sea air. He took a map from the seat pocket in front of him and glanced over it. It showed that the peninsula was much narrower in this part of the Cape, stretching from north to south. To the east was the Atlantic Ocean—there was nothing else between the Cape and Europe!—and to the west was Cape Cod Bay. Benjamin could also see that ponds and salt marshes were scattered across this section of the Cape. He made a mental note to make sure his family explored them after they visited the beach.

His dad turned onto a winding road, and they soon came to the driveway of the inn. It was unlike any place the Baxters had ever stayed before—basically, it was a fabulous old house! It was three stories high, painted yellow and white, with a big turret on one side, a number of stained-glass windows, and a wraparound porch lined with rocking chairs. Lucy and Benjamin followed their parents eagerly up the stairs. "I can't wait to see the room," Lucy said excitedly. "I wonder if we'll get one with a stained-glass window, or maybe one of the round rooms in the turret."

"We'll see," Mrs. Baxter said, chuckling. However, when they walked in, they found that nobody was standing behind the desk. A woman who looked like she might be the innkeeper was talking to a man in a uniform near a staircase.

"In the attic, you said?" the man asked, writing on a notepad. "And how would I get up there?" The innkeeper pointed toward the stairs and then turned to greet the Baxters.

"Hello!" said Benjamin's mom. "I'm Beth Baxter, and I have a reservation for the next two nights . . ."

The innkeeper returned to her place behind the front desk. "Oh, yes," she said. "I'm going to have to move you out of the upstairs rooms on the third floor, because of the investigation . . ." She tapped at her computer keys as she spoke.

"Investigation? Like a police investigation?" Lucy asked, wide-eyed.

The innkeeper laughed. "No, nothing quite that dramatic. It seems we have an animal intruder in our attic! We've been hearing rustling at night, and we need to figure out what's been causing it."

Benjamin only half-listened as his

mom finished checking in and led them upstairs to their room on the second floor. He would do just about anything to be part of the investigation, but he knew better than to ask. The animal in the attic could be dangerous, hungry, or rabid. Still, he really wanted to know what it was!

At the top of the stairs, they entered a suite with a stained-glass window. The kids took one room, their parents took the other, and everyone began unpacking. As Benjamin removed binoculars and walkie-talkies from his bag, he heard loud footsteps clattering down the stairs from the attic, then the voice of the man in the uniform. "You've got to see this!" the man called out to the innkeeper downstairs. When

Benjamin and Lucy popped their heads out of the room, the man said, "It's a colony of big brown bats." Benjamin turned to his parents, and even they looked curious.

"Can we go look?" Lucy and Benjamin asked together.

Mrs. Baxter explained to the man that she and Mr. Baxter were scientists, and the man agreed to show them the bats. Benjamin followed Lucy up the stairs. He'd seen bats in New Mexico, but only from a distance. Here, they'd be up close and personal.

"Be as quiet as you can," his mom said as they followed the man and the innkeeper into the enormous attic. "We don't want to disturb them."

"Don't worry, they're not aggressive

animals," said the man, "in spite of what many people think. But if you want to see them in their quiet state, you need to be quiet yourself."

Benjamin blinked as his eyes adjusted to the darkness. Silently, the man pointed his flashlight toward a corner of the attic ceiling, and at first Benjamin just saw a dark spot. Then he realized he was looking at a group of bats huddled together, hanging upside down by their feet! In the dim beam of light, he could see wings folded over furry brown bodies, and small thin legs clinging to a narrow beam. Benjamin knew that bats hung this way because it was the most efficient way for them to get airborne when they wanted to fly. They had seen a colony of bats when they visited Carlsbad Caverns,

and he remembered that, unlike birds, bats did not have the ability to lift off easily from the ground.

"They're *big* brown bats?" Lucy asked the man. "They don't look that big to me."

"Their wingspan is about a foot

long, and their bodies measure about five inches," the man said. "They're not huge—but they are larger than a related species, the little brown bat. Apart from their size, the two are difficult to tell apart."

"But what are they doing here?" Benjamin asked. "Is something wrong with them? I thought they liked caves . . ."

"Bats choose warm, dark places where they can raise their young," his mom explained. "And sometimes those are places where humans are living, too! They enter houses through spaces under eaves or around chimneys, sometimes even through open windows."

The man added, "They rest during the day, and leave at night through the same openings, flying outdoors to look for insects to eat."

Suddenly something occurred to Benjamin. "Are you going to take them away?" he asked the man. The innkeeper probably didn't want bats living in her attic. But if they didn't live here, what would happen to them? Where would they go?

Before the man could answer, there was a rustling sound. Two of the bats suddenly left their roost and soared out into the room! Benjamin ducked instinctively. He knew they were fairly small, but it felt strange to be in an attic with something flying around. His mom tugged at his sleeve and quickly led both kids toward the door. The man and the innkeeper followed them out and shut the door behind them.

"I will do a bat exclusion," the man explained as he followed the Baxters back down the stairs. "I'll wait until they're all out of the attic, hunting for prey, and then I'll seal the entrances so they can't get back in. They will stay in the neighborhood that they know so well and still be able to find food in familiar places. But they will need to find a new place to live."

"Will we see them again?" Lucy asked. "We're staying here for two nights."

"I don't want to disturb them again," the man said. "But you might see them flying out at dusk, looking for their next meal."

Benjamin wanted to remember the bats, so when they got back to their room, he took out his notebook, drew a quick picture of them, and jotted down some notes. When he was done, he finished unpacking. In the few hours they had left before dinner, the Baxters would be checking out one of the beaches on the Cape Cod National Seashore. They were determined to make the most of their time on the Cape!

"I can't wait to see the beach," Benjamin said excitedly an hour later.

"Me, too. And did you know that Nauset Light Beach is one of the main nesting grounds for the endangered piping plover?" Lucy quizzed her family as they stepped out of their car, just a short distance away from the inn. From the parking lot, they followed a winding path until they spotted a lighthouse and then, around another curve, the open ocean! Benjamin had never seen a beach quite like this one before, nestled below a steep cliff and wide sand dunes. Once he carefully made his way to the bottom, Benjamin could see nothing made by humans except the lighthouse: no cars, no roads, no buildings—only a sweeping stretch of sand and clear blue water.

"Okay, you two. We have only a short time," his dad said. "Pretty soon we'll need to find a place to have dinner. But we can start exploring this afternoon and come back again before we leave Cape Cod."

Benjamin looked at the water and thought about taking a swim . . . until he dipped his feet in. "Yikes!" he said to Lucy. "It's a lot colder than the water back home!"

Lucy grinned at him. "What did you expect?" she asked. "It's the middle of September, and the leaves are starting to change color. It might not feel like fall back home yet, but it's definitely fall here! Do you want to go exploring instead?"

With their parents' permission, the Baxter kids set off down the beach, taking their walkie-talkies so they could radio back if they needed any help.

The tide was going out, and seagulls were swooping down to seize whatever they could find on the newly exposed sand. Where there had been shellfish only recently, there were now just heaps of empty shells. Benjamin even watched a gull snatch a wriggling crab out of a wave! He was wondering how he could learn what kind of gulls these were when Lucy sucked in a breath and stopped him. "Oh, there they are!" she whispered, pointing to something scurrying along the sand. "Piping plovers!"

A pair of small birds ran toward the water on tiny orange legs and stopped.

They stood there for a second, and Benjamin studied their full-bellied bodies, most of which were the same color as the sand except for a band of black across their foreheads and around their necks. The next wave crashed onto the shore, and they quickly scampered up toward drier sand, paused, and began heading for the water again.

"Look how fast they are!" Benjamin said.

"I think they're looking for food," Lucy said. "They eat tiny invertebrates—animals without skeletons—that live in the water. But it seems like they don't want to get wet!" As the kids continued watching, Lucy added, "We're lucky to get to see them. There are fewer than two thousand pairs of piping plovers on the whole Atlantic coast, and parts of this beach are totally closed when they're nesting in the spring."

Above the roar of the waves, Benjamin heard one of the birds call, "*Peep-u!*"

He gave Lucy a funny look. "How do you know so much about the plovers?"

"I read a book about them before we left home," she explained. "They used to be common birds, but their feathers were popular for hats in the eighteen hundreds, and they were hunted until not many were left. When laws made it illegal to hunt them, their numbers bounced back."

Suddenly, the plovers took flight. They were so small that Benjamin's eye couldn't follow them very far, but he figured they'd moved on to another stretch of sand.

"So why are there so few of them now?" Benjamin asked Lucy as they headed back toward their parents.

"Their habitat is the beach," his sister said. "And piping plovers are threatened all the time, even when people just walk across the sand. Because of their color, they're hard to see. And even one wrong footstep can crush a half-buried nest."

Benjamin immediately started to watch where he was stepping. "Don't worry," Lucy said, noticing her brother's careful steps. "Their nesting season is in the spring. We're not going to step on any nests now."

"That's why they're in danger of

becoming extinct?" Benjamin asked. It was hard to believe that a species could disappear just because people were walking on the beach.

Lucy nodded. "They just don't do well living side by side with humans," she said. "And Cape Cod has more people than ever. Not to mention pets. Scientists are doing what they can to bring the plovers back—trying to keep their nests safe and keep dogs off the beach. But there still aren't very many of them."

Suddenly, their walkie-talkies crackled to life. "Benjamin, Lucy, let's go. It's getting late," Mrs. Baxter said.

As they found their parents and walked back up to the car, Benjamin couldn't stop thinking about the birds. The bats they'd seen that morning were being moved out of their home by some humans, but at least they could stay in the neighborhood. The piping plovers, though, had no place to go. It just didn't seem fair! There had to be a balance—a way for humans and animals to live together.

Chapter Four

Benjamin and Lucy couldn't wait to continue exploring the seashore, so the Baxters were back at the beach early the next day, with a stiff wind blowing all around them. Mr. and Mrs. Baxter had arranged for a ranger to guide them on a hike. "Hey!" Lucy yelled as the baseball cap flew off her head.

"Hold onto your hat!" Mrs. Baxter

joked, walking past the wooden fence and the dunes and onto the beach.

Benjamin looked at the whitecaps on the water and the dune grass rippling behind him with each gust of wind. He was glad his family had prepared for the weather, because he didn't want anything to get in the way of the hike they were about to take.

Just as Benjamin looked at his watch, a ranger appeared at the appointed meeting place. "Welcome to the beach! And thanks for coming," he told the Baxters. "My name is Bill, and I lead nature walks in any weather!" He brushed his hair out of his eyes and added, "In some ways, it's best to explore the beach on a blustery day like this, when there are fewer visitors. Wildlife is more likely to come out of hiding without many people around. So let's get started!"

Bill led the Baxters on a path toward the dunes, the region of sand hills and plant life that stretched out behind the beach. "Most people just walk right past the dunes on their way to the water," he said. "But if you stop and look, you'll see that the dunes are a fascinating world all on their own. Their formation is a complex process that plays an important role in beach ecology. Without them, our beaches would be in big trouble."

Benjamin observed the dunes closely as he followed the ranger. Bill was right—he'd never taken much notice of them before, even back home in Florida. In New Mexico, though, his family had visited some stark white gypsum sand dunes in the desert, and he and Lucy had found many animals living there, protecting themselves from the harsh desert climate. He wondered what animals were living here, adapted to this gusty wind.

As another burst of wind swept up, Bill raised his voice and said, "See how the wind is carrying sand from the beach back toward this dune area?" Benjamin ducked his head to look without getting sand in his eyes. Bill continued, "This is the same process that starts dunes forming in the first place. Sand blows in from the shore, swirling around whatever stands in its way, until eventually piles of sand collect where there was driftwood or beach grass or some other obstacle. Eventually, piles upon piles form a dune. And there are many dunes that make up this ecosystem."

Lucy scanned the landscape with curiousity. "But a dune is more than just sand, right? Lots of stuff is growing here."

"That's the difference between a dune and an ordinary pile of sand!" Bill said, smiling. "Hardy plants move in to a new dune, and they put down deep roots that keep the sand in place. As they spread across the dune, they change the environment and make it appealing to other kinds of plant life. Before long, the dune becomes home to many kinds of plants and animals."

Bill stopped at some shrubs lining the path. They were as tall as Benjamin, and had small purple fruit hanging from their branches. "Are these some kind of blueberries?" Benjamin asked, pointing to the berries.

"Good guess, but these are beach plums. They love the sandy soil in dune areas and can tolerate the constant salt spray in the air. Their roots keep the dune sand in place, as I said. But plants like these also serve two other purposes. Anyone want to guess what they are?"

"Shelter for animals!" Lucy blurted out.

"And food for them, too," Benjamin added. It made sense to Benjamin that once plants established themselves on a dune, animals would move in next, seeing the plants as a good source of food.

"That's right. Birds and other animals, like foxes, eat the plums. I can almost guarantee that we will see some wildlife here," Bill said. "But we need to wait and watch quietly. Observe the part of the dune that's closest to you, rather than trying to take it in all at once. If you pay close attention, a whole new world will come into view."

Zipping up his sweatshirt to block out more wind, Benjamin stood on the edge of a dune, several feet away from the rest of his family. From where he was standing, the sky and the Atlantic Ocean seemed so big that it was hard to focus on a tiny corner of his sand dune, where tall grass was swaying in the breeze. Other birds must nest here, he realized, if plover nests could survive out there on the beach. The

tide would bring other creatures close to the dune, too.

Just as he was trying to guess what he might see, he noticed some movement in the sand, near the base of a large rock. Slowly, Benjamin drew closer and stooped down to take a look. It was a snake! It had a brown body with a pattern of black spots along its back, and appeared to be less than two feet long. Benjamin watched curiously as the snake burrowed into the sand with its head. He'd never seen a snake do anything like that before! When the snake's head was practically underground, he risked moving a little. "Mom," he whispered, waving her over. "Come take a look at this!"

Mrs. Baxter tiptoed toward him, saw the burrowing snake, and said softly, "That's an eastern hognose snake. It gets its name from its upturned snout. It's totally harmless, but totally fascinating. It looks like it's burrowing for its favorite food: toads! These snakes are immune to the poisons that the toads make to protect themselves from predators."

Benjamin and his mom watched the

snake emerge from its burrow, empty-mouthed, and slither along the sand to try looking in another place.

Just then, Lucy came up behind them. "What did you find?" she asked, not as quietly as she could have. Suddenly, the snake turned in the direction of Lucy and began hissing loudly and flattening out its head and neck.

Now the harmless snake looked like a cobra!

"Kids, just step back slowly. The eastern hognose snake won't attack. But it doesn't want us around here, either."

As the Baxters cautiously moved back, the snake suddenly twisted around and went limp on the ground. The next thing they knew, the snake's mouth was open and its tongue was hanging out! Benjamin guessed what was happening now. "It's rolling over and playing dead?" he asked his mom.

She grinned. "Just like Daisy!" she said, referring to their dog back in Florida. "But for Daisy, it was only a game. For the snake, it's defense. It sees us as a threat, and this is how it defends itself."

As Bill and Mr. Baxter walked up, Benjamin said, "You won't believe what we just saw! An eastern hognose snake!" He and Lucy turned to show them, but the snake had disappeared for the time being.

Before much longer, Bill was looking at his watch. "Sorry, folks, but I'm just about out of time. Feel free to keep exploring among the dunes, but I need to head back to the visitors' center to meet another group."

As he said his good-byes, Benjamin happened to notice a sign in the sand, saying KEEP OFF THE DUNES. Before Bill walked away, Benjamin said, "Are you sure it's okay if we roam around here alone?" Curious, he pointed to the sign.

Bill smiled. "The sign should really

say 'Stay on the path.' That's the only safe place on the dunes. If people wander around and trample the dunes' plants, eventually their roots will die—and without the roots to stabilize them, the dunes will give way. The same thing happens when people try to build things on the dunes."

"Without the dunes, the animals would be in trouble," Lucy added, frowning.

"Exactly," Bill said, waving goodbye and heading down the beach.

"And that's not all," Mr. Baxter jumped in. "Along with ruining the animals' habitat, builders can harm their *own* habitat. Dunes act as a sort of buffer between the ocean and the land—they keep the water from wearing away at the land, or flooding the land during storms. If you harm the dunes, you're destroying that natural protection."

"So why would anybody ever build on one?" Benjamin asked, puzzled.

"People like to be near the water, just like many other animals," his father said. "But they need to build responsibly. Thoughtless building will destroy animal habitats and eventually ruin the beach, too. Luckily, building practices are changing. It's in nobody's best interest to destroy a dune, after all. There's only so much waterfront for all of us. People, plants, and animals all have to find a way to share."

Chapter Five

Benjamin was thinking about sharing in a totally different way when they sat down at an outdoor picnic table to eat their lunch. He and Lucy had each ordered the same thing from the Snack Shack—grilled cheese and french fries. So why was a hungry seagull picking on *him*? It didn't seem at all bothered that there were other people around—

it plucked a french fry right out of Benjamin's hand. It didn't even mind a little ketchup! Benjamin wrapped his arms around his plate, hoping that would help. He didn't want to share his lunch! And he was pretty sure it wouldn't be good for the seagull, either.

He took a big bite out of his sandwich while the gull was distracted, thinking about the bigger picture for a moment. Was the gull hungry because humans had invaded its territory or taken its food? All species on the Cape depended on each other, whether it was the cod and the lobster or the snake and the toad, and people were one of the species. But it sounded like people weren't really sharing, in spite of what his dad had said. They seemed to be taking more than their part of the land and the fish and the water.

Ben took another bite of his sandwich and was about to ask Lucy what she thought when Mrs. Baxter said, "Okay, kids, we have a fun activity lined up." She grinned enthusiastically as she popped a fried clam in her mouth. "We are going to go digging for clams, Cape Cod style!"

"I'm not sure I want to dig and eat clams," Lucy said skeptically.

Mr. Baxter laughed. "Don't worry, you don't have to eat them; just observe and study them."

Benjamin smiled as he patted the front pocket of his sweatshirt, where his notebook was stuffed. He would have to grab a plastic bag and wrap up his notebook so it wouldn't be damaged by the water. He couldn't wait to start looking for some real, live clams!

A little while later, Benjamin squelched along the edge of the water in his oldest water shoes and an even older T-shirt, which his mom had made him bring from home, probably just for this messy part of the trip. He imagined that earlier in the day, at high tide, this part of Cape Cod Bay had been all sparkling water and early-morning kayakers. Now the water had receded quite a bit, leaving behind a stretch of muddy, rippling sand. Benjamin followed his father over the ripples, but he couldn't help stopping when he came to a large puddle of water left behind when the tide went out. "Hey, look!" he called to Lucy. "A tide pool!"

Back home in Florida, the Baxter kids had seen tide pools filled with starfish and anemones. Here, though, Benjamin saw something totally bizarre when he peeked in. It was an animal he'd never seen before. In fact, it didn't even look like an animal! It had a large, hard shell—it looked almost like a helmet—and a long, spiky tail. As he watched it creep along the bottom of the pool, he realized what he was looking at. "Hey, Lucy, come see this. It's a horseshoe crab!" It moved differently than other crabs, walking forward rather than sideways. It didn't have antennae either, and its shell covered much more of its body than an ordinary crab's would.

When Lucy arrived, she squatted down and watched it intently. "Did you know that horseshoe crabs are some of the oldest creatures on earth? They were living on earth even before the first dinosaurs appeared!"

Benjamin was imagining what the world was like when the horseshoe crab was a new species . . . until his dad called him back into the present. "Don't forget we're looking for clams!" he reminded the kids.

Mr. Baxter was already knee-deep in the water, holding a bucket and what looked like four small pitchforks, which he handed out to Benjamin, Lucy, and Mrs. Baxter. "These are clam rakes," he explained. "They let you dig into the sand to get a clam, but leave the sand behind. Whatever we find, we can put into this bucket," he added.

"But how will we know where to find them?" Lucy asked.

"The best way is to feel the sand with your feet or even your hands," Mr. Baxter said. "We're looking for hard-shelled clams, or quahogs, and they live only a couple of inches beneath the surface. Where there's a quahog underneath, you'll feel something round and hard."

"Coe-hog?" Lucy repeated. "I've never heard of that."

"Like lobsters, there are large numbers of them in the North Atlantic. And if you think their name sounds funny, you should see how it's spelled!" Mr. Baxter squinted at the water, as if looking for the best place to start searching.

Benjamin wasn't sure he would know what a quahog felt like, but he squatted down, put his rake into the water, and ran his hands along the bottom. Within a few minutes, he'd found something pretty solid under the sand. Quickly, he dug a hole around it and scooped it out with his rake. It was a clam! He dipped it back into the water until it was clean.

"I found one!" he called out to the rest of his family, and soon they were gathered around him. Benjamin held the quahog in his hands for all of them to see. It didn't look very dramatic, actually: it was about two inches wide, and its two grayish rounded shells were held together by a hinge at the top. He checked to see if it was open, but the two shells were clamped tightly together.

"See these rings?" his mom asked, pointing to several lines that ran along the shells. "They're like the rings inside a tree's trunk—they show how old the quahog is. About thirty years, it looks like. Older than both of you kids combined! Quahogs grow slowly and live a long time."

Lucy studied it for a second, then said, "I know people eat clams. But how do clams eat? Their shells are closed, so how can anything get in?"

Benjamin was sure they'd seen clams before, either on the beach in Florida or in his mom's lab. Come to think of it, though, he didn't know the answer to this question.

Mrs. Baxter showed her a tiny whitish speck protruding from one edge of the quahog. "It's hard to see without a magnifying glass, but this is a tiny tube that allows a clam to take in water. Once the water is inside the shells, it passes over the clam's gills, which filter out the water and trap the algae the clam needs to survive. Then water passes out through a different tube. A clam can filter about a gallon of water per hour!"

Benjamin turned the quahog over in his hand. It was smaller than most people's wallets—it was amazing to think that the equivalent of a large jug of milk could pass through it in just an hour!

Mrs. Baxter said, "In addition to quahogs, these waters are rich in soft-shelled clams—they have thinner shells, and burrow into tidal mud—as well as mussels and scallops and oysters. Shellfish from the Cape are eaten all over the world."

Lucy frowned. "Are they overfished, too?" she asked.

"Actually, no," her father replied. "There are strict rules about where and when and how shellfish can be harvested, and fishermen need licenses before they begin. The Cape guards its shellfish carefully, so the populations can continue to grow and stay healthy."

Benjamin dipped into the sand again and felt for more quahogs. The lump he thought might be one turned out to be a rock, and then he got distracted by a small plane flying over the water. Probably carrying other visitors, he thought. He wondered what it was like to see the bay from above. As Benjamin watched the plane fade away into the distance, he noticed something stirring on the water's surface, close to the horizon.

His backpack was in the car, but he'd brought his binoculars in case there were any interesting birds to watch. They were strapped around his neck and tucked under his old T-shirt for protection. Benjamin took them out and focused on where he'd seen the movement. For a moment, he saw only a huge expanse of water—then he saw some splashing and the flash of a gray body leaping out!

Could it be a whale? he wondered. Maybe he would finally see one! But quickly, he realized that a whale wouldn't come so close to shore. The water would be too shallow for such a massive creature. So maybe it was a dolphin? There was another splash, another leap, another flash. Benjamin took another look through his binoculars and followed the splashing toward a small, rocky island he hadn't noticed before. There, a seal was flopping onto the rocks and settling down to rest in the sun.

"Look everyone!" he called out to the rest of his family. "A seal!"

The Baxters passed around the binoculars to take a closer look.

"I think it's a harbor seal," said Mrs. Baxter.

"That would make sense," said Mr. Baxter. "There's a large population of

them in New England, and they usually stay close to shore." He peered at the seal and passed the binoculars back to Benjamin. "Yes—take a look at its gray spots and round head. Definitely a harbor seal. And there are probably more seals out there as well—harbor seals tend to congregate in groups."

Benjamin grinned. He was proud that he'd been the one to spot the seal. His parents were always talking about observing the world closely, and doing that had totally paid off this afternoon. A seal was cool, no doubt about it. But a whale would have been even cooler. And his time on the Cape was running out!

Chapter Six

Sunday arrived too quickly for Benjamin. He felt like he was just beginning to learn about the Cape, and now he had to go back home to Florida. But the Baxters still had a couple of hours before their ferry to Boston and their plane trip home. So Ben and Lucy asked to take one last hike, and their parents agreed.

Now Mr. and Mrs. Baxter lagged

behind as Benjamin followed Lucy on a winding path through a pine forest, taking deep breaths of the clean, cool air. Fall was already underway on Cape Cod, but the weather would still be hot when he returned to Florida. The worst part of it, he thought, was going to school when it still felt so much like summer! A part of him wished he could stay on the Cape a little longer, so he could see the leaves continue to change colors. New England was famous for that, he remembered.

Ahead of him, Lucy was walking up an incline. "Hey, Lucy, wait up!" he shouted. Benjamin checked for his parents before he followed her. The rule was that they had to be in sight at all times, but that didn't mean they had to be close. Through the thick growth of trees, Benjamin could see his father's red T-shirt and his mom's yellow baseball cap off in the distance. Satisfied, he quickly followed his sister up the hill.

At the top, where Lucy had stopped, there was a small clearing and a big view! "Wow! I had no idea we were near any water," he said breathlessly. As he looked out, he found himself looking down at a round lake. Two canoes paddled near the middle of it, and shadows danced on the surface of the clear blue water. He felt as if they'd stumbled upon somebody's secret hideaway.

Peering at her trail map, Lucy said, "It's a kettle pond!"

Benjamin hated to admit it, but he had no idea what that was. Seeing the question on his face, Lucy read aloud from the back of the map. "It says here that when the last glaciers left Cape Cod twelve thousand years ago, they left behind huge chunks of ice. When those ice chunks melted, the ground beneath them collapsed, making huge holes in the earth that eventually collected the water. Unlike other ponds, there are no streams running in or out of kettle ponds."

"So they date back to the Ice Age? Wow!" said Benjamin. "And . . . what animals live in them?"

Lucy grinned. "I think we still have time to find out!"

Together, they studied the map to find the best path down to the water, and this time Benjamin took the lead. His parents were still in the distance,

and Lucy fell a bit behind when she stopped to find some trail mix in her backpack. Benjamin was pretty much alone when there was a rustling in the trees to his right. As he turned, he saw a deer quickly run across the path!

It was about three feet tall, Benjamin guessed, with a grayish-brown coat.

Probably a female, since it had no antlers. Its tail was standing up, and he could see a flash of white on its underside. Benjamin was pretty sure he was looking at a white-tailed deer! They were common across North America, he knew, even though people had once hunted them intensely. The deer moved quickly out of sight, so fast that he didn't get a chance to call Lucy or his parents over.

When everyone caught up with him, he announced, "I just saw a white-tailed deer!"

"Really? You could see the white?" his dad asked. "Underneath the tail?"

Benjamin nodded. "It was sticking up," he said.

"That's what white-tails do when

they're alarmed," his dad said, looking around. "Makes you wonder what's after it, doesn't it?"

"It could be a fox," his mom said. "We should be careful as we make our way down to the pond!"

They hiked down to the edge of the water. From here, he could see that what he'd thought were shadows on the water were actually lily pads, drying up like old leaves even though they were in the pond. Summer was their season, and now they were at the end of their life cycle. There was a sandy beach, in a ring almost all the way around the pond, but Lucy was crouched down among some weeds near the trail, looking at something on the ground. "Come quick!" she said. "A turtle!"

"What's the rush?" joked Benjamin.
"It's not like it's going to run away!"
He made his way through the weeds
ahead of his parents, though. He was
just as excited as Lucy to see it.

The turtle was pretty small—maybe
five inches, Benjamin guessed. It had
a high, domed shell, covered with an
intricate pattern of brown and yellow and green. Its legs were yellow,

too, with a different pattern on them, and its eyes were bright red! Lucy was watching it munch on some purple berries, and the turtle didn't seem at all disturbed by her presence.

When their parents crept up, Lucy asked, "What kind is it, do you think?"

Mrs. Baxter had an answer right away. "It's an eastern box turtle," she replied softly. "It can completely retract its arms and head into its shell until it looks like a box! In a few weeks it will start preparing to hibernate— turtles burrow into the ground for the winter. For now, though, it looks like this one is just having a snack."

"Does it live in the pond?" Lucy asked.

"No, box turtles live mostly on

land," her mom continued. "But occasionally they'll go for a quick swim on a hot day. This one probably likes the pond habitat because it provides many places to keep out of the sun: rocks and plants and heaps of dead leaves. Plus, there's lots of food in and around the pond, like worms, insects, mushrooms, and berries. Box turtles will eat almost anything!"

"Right now, I'd eat almost anything," Mr. Baxter said, chuckling. "Let's head back so we have time for a snack before we go to the ferry." Much as they all wanted to stay, it was time to begin their long trip back home.

Later that day, Benjamin stood on the deck of the ferry, watching the shoreline of Cape Cod fade away. On family trips, he usually took tons of notes and tried to record every new experience in his notebook. This trip was a little different, though. He'd done more watching than writing this time. Sometimes, he was starting to think, it was possible to miss some details because you were so busy writing other ones down! Because of this trip, he now had a better sense of how everything fit together, plant life and animal life, plus the people and the landscape.

But there was one thing missing from his experience in Cape Cod. He'd seen Woods Hole, the world-famous center for the study of marine biology, and he'd seen many of the animals that Cape Cod was known for. The biggest one, though, was the one he hadn't managed to lay eyes on.

Woods Hole, like many other villages on the Cape, had started out as a harbor for whaling ships. But where were the whales? Benjamin wondered. He supposed he'd have to wait till next time to see one, just as he'd have to wait to see the rest of the kettle pond, but it was hard to predict when his family would return to Cape Cod.

A small boat zoomed by the ferry at high speed, spraying up water as it passed. Benjamin watched it go by, and noticed the foamy wake that formed in its path. At first he didn't even think it was strange that water was still shooting into the air from the surface—he figured it had something to do with the boat. But when the boat had been out of view for several minutes and the spraying continued, Benjamin gripped the ferry's railing more tightly. "Hey, guys!" he said, never taking his eyes off the water. "I think there's something next to the ferry!"

Lucy and Mr. and Mrs. Baxter rushed over to Benjamin and looked where he was pointing. There was another spray, then nothing, then another spray, then nothing, several times. Could it be? Benjamin wondered. Just when he was giving up on ever seeing it, there was a mighty splash as a huge figure rose out of the water. A whale! It was longer and thinner than the humpback Benjamin had seen in

Alaska, and it had a big white patch on the side of its jaw. "A fin whale?" he asked his dad. (Since he'd seen the humpback, Benjamin had learned the differences among the many kinds of whales.) His father nodded, offering no more information, but Benjamin knew it was the second-largest whale—

the second-largest creature—on earth! The Baxters watched in wonder as the whale dove down, disappeared, then came back to the surface. It let out vapor through its blowhole several times, then popped out of the water again before its next dive!

Benjamin didn't know what to do. He wanted to watch for as long as he possibly could. But he also wanted to dig out his notebook and write down everything about this unexpected end to their trip! Seeing the whale brought the whole trip together, he thought. One of the largest animals on earth was diving into the ocean to eat krill, tiny crustaceans that are some of the world's smallest. There was no better example of the way different animal species depended on each other, he realized.

He watched until the ferry passed the whale, then wrote and sketched until the ferry stopped in Boston. His family's trip to the Cape had been amazing, but seeing the whale made it complete. As he wrote his findings in his notebook, he thought to himself that this had been one of the best trips he'd ever been on!

JEFF CORWIN has worked for the conservation of endangered species and ecosystems around the globe. He is the host of a variety of popular television shows, including Animal Planet's *Jeff Corwin Experience*, *Corwin's Quest*, *Spring Watch*, and *King of the Jungle*; Disney's *Going Wild with Jeff Corwin*; *Investigation Earth* with the Discovery Networks; NBC's *Jeff Corwin Unleashed*, which was nominated four times for an Emmy and won an Emmy for an Outstanding Host; and the Travel Channel's *Into Alaska* and *Into the American West*. His popular television series are seen in 120 countries worldwide. He also cocreated and cohosted CNN's *Planet in Peril* with Anderson Cooper in 2007. *Men's Journal* recognized Jeff as the world's greatest host of a natural history series. In 2008, Jeff Corwin was named Ambassador of Climate Change for one of the nation's leading conservation organizations, Defenders of Wildlife. And in 2009, Jeff Corwin began hosting a new series for The Food Network entitled *Extreme Cuisine*, about unusual and interesting food from around the world. He also produced and hosted *100 Heartbeats*, a groundbreaking series for NBC that highlights Earth's most endangered species along with the conservation heroes trying to save them. *100 Heartbeats* has also been made into a book of the same name.

A native of Massachusetts, Jeff has established an interactive museum and environmental education center called the EcoZone. Based in Norwell, Massachusetts, the EcoZone strives to build awareness for the wildlife and ecology unique to the wetlands of southeastern Massachusetts. When not traveling the world, Jeff can be found at his home off the coast of Massachusetts, where he lives with his wife and two daughters.